LETTERS TO THE LADY UPSTAIRS

MARCEL PROUST

Letters to the Lady Upstairs

TRANSLATED AND WITH AN AFTERWORD
BY LYDIA DAVIS

Text edited and annotated
by Estelle Gaudry and Jean-Yves Tadié
with a foreword by Jean-Yves Tadié

4th Estate • London

4th Estate
An imprint of HarperCollins *Publishers*
1 London Bridge Street
London SE1 9GF
www.4thestate.co.uk

First published in Great Britain by 4th Estate in 2017
First published in the United States by New Directions in 2017
First published in France as *Lettres à sa voisine* by Éditions Gallimard in 2013

Published by arrangement with Éditions Gallimard.
4th Estate is grateful to Éditions Gallimard for providing the facsimiles
and photographs, and for facilitating their use in this edition.

Facsimiles of Proust's letters are courtesy of a
private collection / Musée des Lettres et Manuscrits, Paris
Photographs on front and back endpapers and page 35 are
courtesy of the Gérard Emler collection

A catalogue record for this book is available from the British Library

ISBN 978-0-00-826289-1

Printed and bound by CPI Group (UK) Ltd, Croydon, CR0 4YY

MIX
Paper from
responsible sources
FSC™ C007454

This book is produced from independently certified FSC paper
to ensure responsible forest management.

For more information visit: www.harpercollins.co.uk/green

Table of contents

Foreword

The present collection forms a real novel in miniature, and is the result of a surprise discovery: twenty-three letters written to a certain lady of whom at first we knew nothing, along with three to her husband. She turned out to have been Marcel Proust's neighbour on the third floor of 102 Boulevard Haussmann, one Mme Marie Williams, the wife of an American dentist. Doctor Charles D. Williams's dental practice was two floors above the mezzanine – that is, directly above the head of poor Marcel. And that was the source of more than one drama endured by that noise-phobic.

We know very little about her. Born Marie Pallu in 1885, she married first, in 1903, a certain Paul Emler, who worked for a maritime insurance company. With him she had a son in 1904 whom Proust knew. She divorced in July 1908, the year in which she moved into the building on Boulevard Haussmann. The dentist was her second husband (though not the last). Through Proust's letters, she appears to us like a heroine in a Maupassant novel, perhaps *Our Hearts*, for instance – we know that that novel was inspired by Proust's friend Mme Geneviève Straus, also a friend of Mme Williams, who, oddly, resembled her, as she also resembled the courtesan Laure Hayman, a model for Proust's character Odette (as though, with her, Proust were testing the theory according to which one always loves the same type of woman).

We know what Proust's housekeeper Céleste Albaret said about the couple: on the floor above, 'there was that extraordinary man Williams, the American dentist. [. . .] Williams was a sports enthusiast and went off every Saturday with his chauffeur to play golf. He had married an artist, very distinguished, very perfumed, who was a great admirer of Monsieur Proust and had told him so in her letters. I recall that she played the harp. Her apartment was on the third floor, above her husband's office. M. Proust's opinion was that they formed a "disparate" couple. I don't think he knew Mme Williams, but they corresponded and I know that he rather liked her refined way of expressing herself in her letters.'[1]

In this epistolary novel, the two correspondents compete in style: 'Through a grace of generosity – or a play of reflections – you lend my letters some of the qualities of your own. Yours are delicious, delicious in heart, spirit, style, "talent",' writes Proust to Mme Williams, whose letters we do not have (as we do not have those of others of Proust's correspondents, pages that were no doubt the victims of some sad auto-da-fé). What is intriguing is that these letters were exchanged between neighbours, from one floor to the other, sometimes even via the post. In each of them, Proust deployed all his charm towards Mme Williams, his sparkling humour, his cultivation, his skill with a compliment. Beyond his desire to please a neighbour who had some control over the silence he so needed, he felt a real sympathy for this other recluse, a

---

The notes can be found at the end of the book, beginning on page 69.

kind of affection, as though, invisible yet present, she played the maternal role of that other ailing woman, Mme Straus.

What were the letters about? The noise first of all, the work being done on the floor above, which tormented Proust during the hours when he was sleeping and writing. 'How right I was to be discreet when you wanted me to investigate whether the morning noise was coming from a sink. What was that compared to those hammers? "A shiver of water on moss" as Verlaine says of a song "that weeps only to please you".' In fact, Proust set each of his remarks within a humorous comparison that also achieved one more degree of art. For everything makes noise, even painters, who sing like a certain famous tenor: 'Generally a painter, a house painter especially, believes he must cultivate at the same time as the art of Giotto that of Reszke. This one is quiet while the electrician bangs. I hope that when you return you will not find yourself surrounded by anything less than the Sistine frescoes ...'

Music was also one of his subjects, because Mme Williams loved music and played the harp (perhaps also the piano): 'Clary told me what a great musician you were. Will I never be able to come up and hear you? The Franck quartet, the *Béatitudes*, the Beethoven Quartets (all music that I have in fact here) are the objects of my most nostalgic desire.'

Proust, who described the hawthorns or the young girls in flower, admirer of *Parsifal*, with its flower-maidens and its 'Enchantment of Good Friday', placed flowers at the heart of his friendship and his correspondence. He sent bouquets to the young woman, and he delivered a dazzling speech on autumn roses in poetry. He was aware of being heir to the literary tradition of the language of flowers. He felt that 'all women are tinted with the blood of roses'.[2] They recur in the title of the second volume of *In Search of Lost Time*, which Proust was just then writing. He demonstrated his knowledge of poetry yet again in creating a pastiche, from memory, of the whole of the once celebrated sonnet by Félix Arvers (cited in *Search*). It is amusing to see that in *The Guermantes Way* Proust attributes this taste for quoting poetry to the footman Périgot, who, writing to peasants 'whose stupefaction he anticipated [. . .], intermingled his own reflections with Lamartine's verses, as though he were saying: time will tell, or even: hello'.

Memory, in fact, was never very far away: 'When one is endowed with imagination, as you are, one possesses all the landscapes one has loved, and this is the inalienable treasure of the heart. But really a home where you have memories of your family, a home which you cannot see except through reveries which recede into the distant past, is a very moving thing.' It was the memory of beauty that allowed these two infirm people to endure the ugliness that surrounded them. Proust was ill, and so was Mme Williams, who must not have been very happy with her often absent husband. We see her going off to take the cure at Bagnoles-de-l'Orne. Or: 'It saddens me very much to learn that you are ill. If bed does not bore you too much I believe that in itself it exerts a very sedative effect on the kidneys. But perhaps you are bored (though it seems to me [*word skipped: difficult?*] to be bored with you). Couldn't I send you some books. Tell me what would distract you, I would be so pleased.' And, one summer, from Cabourg:

'It seems natural to me that I should be ill. But at least illness ought to spare Youth, Beauty and Talent!'

In the depths of illness lies solitude: it is unusual to see Proust offering his company to a solitary woman (letter 18). His letters, which take to an extreme the art of insinuating himself into others' hearts and minds, might have inspired jealousy in the husband. However, the misfortunes of the times came to outweigh them: the war, with its sorrows and its destruction. Reflecting this, for instance, is the very beautiful letter 25 about the bombing of the Reims Cathedral. Mme Williams had had a book delivered to Proust which we can identify as A. Demar-Latour's *Ce qu'ils ont détruit: La cathédrale de Reims bombardée et incendiée en septembre 1914* [What they destroyed: The cathedral of Reims bombed and burned in September 1914] (see note 52). Proust comments on it after offering the opinion that the sculptures of Reims are both the heir of Greek antiquity and the heralds of Leonardo da Vinci's smile: 'But I who insofar as my health permits make to the stones of Reims pilgrimages as piously awestruck as to the stones of Venice believe I am justified in speaking of the diminution to humanity that will be consummated on the day when the arches that are already half burnt away collapse forever on those angels who without troubling themselves about the danger still gather marvellous fruits from the lush stylized foliage of the forest of stones.' Worse than the destruction of stones is the death of men, and in witness to this is a very beautiful letter of condolence to Mme Williams in which Proust mentions the death of Bertrand de Fénelon, of which he speaks in all his letters of this period and which will be represented in the novel by the death of Robert de Saint-Loup, before he speaks to her of the death of her brother: 'I myself have only an experience of sadness that is already very old and almost uninterrupted.'

Mme Williams took an interest in Proust's writing. He was therefore careful to explain to her that it was not enough to have read *Swann's Way* and the excerpts of the next volume published in *La Nouvelle Revue Française* in 1914 if she were to understand his novel. 'But will these detached pages give you an idea of the 2nd volume? And the 2nd volume itself doesn't mean much; it's the 3rd that casts the light and illuminates the designs of the rest. But when one writes a work in 3 volumes in an age when publishers want only to publish one at a time, one must resign oneself to not being understood, since the ring of keys is not in the same part of the building as the locked doors.' He also wanted her to know that the characters appeared very different from what they would be in the next volume, very different from what they were in reality. And he takes up, again, the example of Baron de Charlus, whom one believes to be Odette's lover, whereas Swann is right to entrust him with his mistress (since Charlus is not attracted to women). And yet, he is also wrong, Proust declares, in a second reversal: Odette is the only woman with whom Charlus will have slept (a feature that in fact will not be retained in the final text of the novel and that was perhaps inspired in Proust by the brief and dramatic affair between Montesquiou and Sarah Bernhardt). One has to grasp the overall design of the book, says Proust, which is not possible unless one knows the content of the two following volumes (actually, *The Guermantes Way* and *Time Found Again*: at this stage of the composition, Proust believed he would be able to confine himself to a novel in three volumes).

And what of the husband – the absent figure in this comedy? The *terzo incomodo*? The dentist, who moved his practice to Deauville during the summer months, makes an appearance in *In the Shadow of Young Girls in Flower*, described in this way by Albertine: 'That little old fellow with the dyed hair and yellow gloves, well, he's nicely turned out, not bad looking, he's the Balbec dentist, a good guy.' It is extraordinary to see how Proust allows nothing of his own life to be wasted. One might well suppose, then, that one could put a real name to each character, a real event to each event in his fiction.

Another figure often neglected by Proust's biographers appears here, and that is Clary, an old friend of his and a descendant of a family linked to Napoleon. He was also a friend of Mme Williams. He was ill, and went blind (Proust was to use this feature for Charlus as an old man), and found solace in his religious faith, a fact emphasized by Proust in terms we don't find elsewhere: 'I have learned through some friends very dear to him one thing which I tell you in *confidence* for it is a very delicate subject but one which makes me very happy because I believe that this may be for him a great consolation: I mean an awakening of a profoundly religious life, *an ardent* and profound faith.'

The tone of the letters is that of friendship, of ever growing intimacy, between two solitary people. Proust expresses the wish to go upstairs to the upper floor to listen to music, and he did go up at least once,[3] took an interest in the

Williamses' young son (born in 1904; Proust watched him grow up, took pleasure in his visits, wanted to give him presents), and in Mme Williams's health, and he lavished little comforts on her.

Lovely metaphors, and emotion, and irony, and rhythm: these are the letters of a great writer. We are induced to change our mind about Proust's correspondence. When the first edition of the *Correspondance générale* [General correspondence] was published in six small volumes, edited first by Robert Proust and Paul Brach, and then, for volume 6, by Suzy Mante-Proust (with the assistance of Philip Kolb), between 1930 and 1936, there were cries of sycophancy, frivolous attachment to materiality, snobbery, and, finally, tedium. Some critics even imagined that it would be enough to read a selection. The truth is that, to an unimaginable degree, Proust puts himself in the place of the person whom he is addressing, pushing divination to the point of total fusion. He experiences the feelings of the other before the latter himself has become entirely aware of them; he imagines and feels better than does his interlocutor. He interrupts him to speak in his place.

We do not have the last letters sent to Mme Williams by Proust. Might they have contained touching farewells? Will they resurface one day like so many others, after having slumbered in unknown collections? The dentist left Boulevard Haussmann at the same time as Proust. Constrained to leave by the sale of the building, he moved on May 31, 1919. Proust did not talk to anyone about Mme Williams. As for her, she met a sad end: after divorcing the dentist, she married the great pianist Alexander Brailowsky, thus fulfilling a love of music that the dentist could hardly satisfy except with the sound of his drill. Then, in 1931, in a last and tragic piece of drama, she committed suicide. It had been a long time since Proust was there to make her laugh and comfort her.

As it stands, this dialogue, of which we can hear only one voice, being obliged to reconstruct the other from its reflection, its echo, has the beauty of those damaged statues on the Reims Cathedral as they were described by Proust, when he was sent their photograph by his neighbour.

JEAN-YVES TADIÉ

A note on the French edition

These letters were placed in the collection of the Musée des Lettres et Manuscrits [Museum of Letters and Manuscripts] by the grandson of Mme Williams several years before its doors were closed in late 2014.

Like most of Proust's letters, they are not dated. We have therefore chosen to order them in the way that seemed the most logical, being guided to a certain extent by the development of the friendship and allusions to the work being done in the building, the sending of flowers, the war, Joachim Clary, and Proust's publications. These have allowed us to propose hypothetical dates.

We have respected Proust's orthography, with the exception of his abbreviations. Words underlined by him are printed in italics, as are the titles of works.

A note on the English-language edition

In the light of some new information that became available during the preparation of this translation, the dating and order of some of the letters have been changed from what they were in the French edition, as have, consequently, the order and numbering of the endnotes. The English-language edition will therefore not match the French edition at every point, for those who may have both and want to compare.

1

Madame,

Your letters are 'Parthian Letters'. You give me so great a desire, and almost your permission, to see you: and then at the very moment that I receive the letter, you have left! My most ardent hope is that the coming year may bring the softening, I won't say the forgetting since memory is the proud treasure of wounded hearts, of the trials which the year that is ending has brought you. In this hope I include with you the Doctor, whom I do not know, but whose praises I hear sung by Madame Straus, by everyone.[4] *And very particularly your son who had promised to express his desires to me* so that I could satisfy them and whose discretion, please tell him, is not at all friendly. Please accept Madame my gratitude for your kind concern for my rest, my most respectful greetings.

MARCEL PROUST

2

Madame,

I thank you with all my heart for your beautiful and good letter and *come to ask you on the contrary to allow all possible noise to be made starting now*. I had in fact not anticipated a shortness of breath so severe that it prevents me from trying to sleep. Noise will therefore not bother me in the least (and will be all the more relief for me on a day on which I could rest).[5] It saddens me very much to learn that you are ill. If bed does not bore you too much I believe that in itself it exerts a very sedative effect on the kidneys. But perhaps you are bored (though it seems to me [*word skipped: difficult?*] to be bored with you). Couldn't I send you some books. Tell me what would distract you, I would be so pleased. Don't speak of annoying neighbours, but of neighbours so charming (an association of words contradictory in principle since Montesquiou claims that most horrible of all are 1st neighbours 2nd the smell of post offices) that they leave the constant tantalizing regret that one cannot take advantage of their neighbourliness.[6]

Be so good Madame as to recall me to the Doctor and accept my respectful and grateful greetings.

MARCEL PROUST

Despite the gloomy days, would some flowers please you. And 'which' as Verlaine says?

1 heure

Madame,

Je vous remercie de tout mon
cœur de votre belle et bonne
lettre et viens vous demander
au contraire de la [me] faire
à partir de maintenant tout le
bruit que vous pourrez. J'avais
compté en effet sans une oppression
si vive qu'elle m'empêche d'échapper

3

Dear Monsieur,

I beg you please to present to Madame Williams with all my respect these flowers which without wearying you with vain speeches will convey my gratitude for the delicate goodness which you employ with regard to me and of which I would ask you to find here the most sincere and most distinguished expression.

MARCEL PROUST

I absolutely expect you to tell me what I owe you for the expenses I occasion you by these shifts in the workers' hours.

4

Madame,

I envy your beautiful memories. No doubt that magnificent home which reminds one of Combourg in a less sombre site but which certainly has its poetry too, is not the only one that belongs to you. When one is endowed with imagination, as you are, one possesses all the landscapes one has loved, and this is the inalienable treasure of the heart. But really a home where you have memories of your family, a home which you cannot see except through reveries which recede into the distant past, is a very moving thing. I do not know Bagnoles but I so love Normandy that it is, I think, very pleasant.[7] And then like all those who are ill I have learned to spend my life surrounded by ugliness where through an irony of fate, I am generally in less bad health. I hope Bagnoles does you good, I also hope that you have with you your son whom I regret not having seen in Paris. You are very good to think of the noise. It has been moderate up to now and relatively close to silence. These days a plumber has been coming every morning from 7 to 9; this is no doubt the time he had chosen. I cannot say that in this my preferences agree with his! But he has been very tolerable, and really *everything* has been. Please accept Madame my respectful greetings and sincere obeisance.

MARCEL PROUST

I hope you have good news of the Doctor, I beg you to remember me to him.

5

Madame,

Alas your note sought me in Paris and reaches me in Cabourg . . . just as I am getting into the train! Otherwise, since my incessant attacks find in this air an abatement which causes me to seek it out, I would have tried to go and thank you for your charming letter. I would have tried and I do not flatter myself with the hope that I would have succeeded, knowing from experience how impossible it has been for me to receive very dear friends, come from quite far away to see me. But still I would have made the attempt. I am saddened to learn that you, too, have been suffering. It seems natural to me that I should be ill. But at least illness ought to spare Youth, Beauty and Talent! At least you have the support of a loving heart! I hope with all my heart that you will be completely healthy this year and I beg you Madame, in asking you please to remember me to Doctor Williams, to accept for yourself my most respectful greetings.

MARCEL PROUST

Excuse this letter written at the moment of getting into the train.

6

Dear Monsieur,

I am sending you my little (and very old!) *Portraits of Painters*.[8] You have them already in my illustrated volume *Pleasures and Days* (I think you have received it, not through the post like the Ruskin, it must have been conveyed to you by hand) but the music is very difficult to read in the book, and is much better engraved in these little pieces into which, if Madame Williams, whose admirable talent I know, is curious to cast a glance, she will not be unpleasantly bothered as in the book, by the rather fuzzy look of the fac simile [*sic*]. Today's fog is provoking in me such attacks that I scarcely have the strength to trace these words, so that I'm afraid I will be even more illegible than the musical fac-similes [*sic*]. It is this that is preventing me, exhausted by suffering and having wanted all the same before trying to rest a little in the evening to send up to you the pieces which I have received only just now, so late, from expressing to you the thanks which I owe you for a charming letter already a little old to which I would have liked to respond in a manner a little more detailed, but I am enduring at the moment such bad days that I am a very bad correspondent. Always prepared however to respond to you with exactness if you had something to ask me.

Please be so kind as to accept Monsieur the expression of my very devoted feelings.

MARCEL PROUST

[autumn 1909?]
102 Boulevard Haussmann

Monsieur,

As I so often expose you to the effects of my troubles by asking you when my asthma attacks are too intense to procure me a little silence, – I think it is only fair that when I have something agreeable I ask you to share it with me. I hope that you will be willing to accept these four pheasants with as much simplicity as I put into offering them to you as neighbour. I will also permit myself to send you a few of my works. Unfortunately my articles from the *Figaro* are not yet collected in books and it is perhaps this that would most have interested you.[9] But I will be able meanwhile to present you with the rest. I implore your help for *Monday* the 19th the day after tomorrow. I must make the great effort to try to go out in the evening and as I have attacks of asthma all night long, if in the morning there is hammering above me it's all over for the whole day for resting, my attack will not stop and my evening out is impossible.

Please accept, Monsieur, the expression of my highest regards.

MARCEL PROUST

8

Marcel Proust begs Madame Williams to be so kind as to accept his respectful and enchanted thanks, for the beautiful and artistic letter which she has had the grace and has done him the honour of writing to him. He would be most grateful to her if she would be his spokeswoman with the Doctor to request that there not be too much noise tomorrow Saturday, since he has to go out for a while in the evening. He will not fail as soon as his friend Mr Hahn is back from Aix la Chapelle where he has gone to conduct Prométhée to communicate to him the gracious praise.[10]

Vendredi

Marcel Proust
prie Madame Williams
de vouloir bien accepter ses
respectueux remerciements
sous le charme, pour la
belle lettre d'artiste qu'
elle a eu la grâce de lui
a fait p[er]sonnement de lui
écrire. Il lui serait bien

Il connaissait ant d'être son
interprète auprès du docteur
pour ne pas avoir trop de
... demain Samedi,
devait sortir en Monet
le voir. Il ne manque
pas dit que son ami Mr ?
Hahn sera revenu d'
Aix la Chapelle où il est
allé conduire Prométhée de
lui communiquer la gracieuse
louange...

9

[October 1914?]

Madame,

It is always a very great pleasure for me to receive a letter from you. The latest was particularly sweet for me in these terrible times in which one trembles for all those one loves, and I do not mean by that only those one knows. It is however permitted without being too selfish to have exceptional worries, and the fate of my brother who is operating in the line of fire, has had his hospital bombed, the shells falling even on the operating table so that he has been obliged to take his wounded down into the cellars, is particularly close to my heart. Happily he has been completely safe up to now and has been mentioned in the army's *ordre du jour*.[11] I hope that you too have good news of your family. As for me I will imminently be going before the military service review board. I don't know if I will be taken or not. I had wanted to write you last summer to hear your news. But even well before the War I was overwhelmed with worries. First, I was more or less completely ruined, which I found extremely painful. But shortly afterwards my poor secretary was drowned by falling from an aeroplane into the sea.[12] And the immense sorrow I felt, and that still endures, has prevented me from thinking about material troubles, very small next to an emotional trial. You knew him perhaps by sight because he lived in my home with his wife. But what you could not know is the superior intelligence which was to his, and extremely spontaneous since he had had no schooling, having been until then a simple mechanic. Never did I better understand the profoundness of the saying 'The Spirit bloweth where it listeth.'[13] The part of your letter in which you spoke of Clary is not that part which gave me the least pleasure, pleasure mingled with pain since you tell me he is still unwell.[14] He is a truly rare person, I have a very profound affection for him; I think he does not believe it because for reasons which involve on my part more delicacy than he supposes, I have not expressed it to him. But there is no one whose company I have found sweeter. I never see him and I think constantly of him. I do not know if he has received my book, I sent it to him when it appeared (this is not a reproach for the fact that he has not written to me, he is unwell and excused for everything). But I do not know if the address was correct. And my memory is so fatigued by my drugs that I cannot even manage to specify whether that book did not come back to me, or if it is a hallucination of memory. In any case what I am sure of, is that I sent it. Often I would like to write for very selfish reasons. [*Word missing*] to speak of his health. I'm afraid [*of*] failing to mention a regimen [. . .] that would perhaps very quickly restore [*his*] health. I have known people who [. . .] spoiled their lives, always prey [*to*] attacks of rheumatism until the day [*when some*] astonishingly simple prescriptions [. . .] rigorously observed relieved them and made them regret the time they had lost.[15] I would like to know if before treating himself, Clary saw, even once, a great 'diagnostician'. For example Doctor Faisans.[16] I know Clary to be very withdrawn, very reserved, and it is this that has stopped me from speaking to him about that. But since you speak to me about his health, you will give me great pleasure if you tell him that it concerns me very much. I hope that your own is completely good Madame. The Doctor was good enough to leave his card one day at Cabourg. Would you have the extreme goodness to tell him that starting on that day I tried to go and find him at ~~Deauville~~ Trouville. But automobiles could not go out after 6 o'clock. And I could not manage to leave early enough. One day I succeeded, but on that day it was impossible to find an automobile. If I had not had the plan to go to see him postponed day after day, I would have written to him right [*end of the letter is missing*]

10

Madame,

Please permit me to appeal to you and the Doctor for tomorrow Tuesday regarding the noise (early). I had to go out today in extremely dangerous health conditions and I very much dread tomorrow. —. If in a little while I am better I would be happy to talk to you about Clary. I have learned through some friends very dear to him one thing which I tell you in *confidence* for it is a very delicate subject but one which makes me very happy because I believe that this may be for him a great consolation: I mean an awakening of a profoundly religious life, *an ardent* and profound faith.

   Your very respectful

MARCEL PROUST

About Clary, I ask you not to speak of this at least for the moment.

11

Night of Wednesday to Thursday

Madame,

Through the grace of generosity – or a play of reflections – you lend my letters some of the qualities possessed by your own. Yours are delicious, delicious in heart, in spirit, in style, in 'talent'. —. The continuation of *Swann* (if I have properly understood)? or *Swann* itself? If it is the continuation, there exist only the excerpts, very long, true, of the 2nd volume, which appeared in the N^lle Revue F^çaise.[17] The War came, the 2nd and 3rd volumes could not be published, naturally. I have friends who continue to write books, and publish them, since they send them to me. No doubt their publisher is not mobilized like mine, their thoughts are not mobilized like mine which, as regards 'proofs' [*épreuves*, which also means 'trials, difficulties'], are at this time turned towards others than those I would have to be correcting. So if it is the continuation of Swann I have only the excerpts from the N^lle R. F. This took up two Issues of the Revue. I should have them. But where? I will look for them. If I don't find them today, I will write to Gide, the only director of the N.R.F. who has been mobilized in Paris itself (as far as I know). I am too happy about having such a reader as you to miss this opportunity. But will these detached pages give you an idea of the 2nd volume? And the 2nd volume itself doesn't mean much; it's the 3rd that casts the light and illuminates the plans of the rest. But when one writes a work in 3 volumes in an age when publishers want only to publish one at a time, one must resign oneself to not being understood, since the ring of keys is not in the same part of the building as the locked doors. —. It is true that one must resign oneself to something worse which is to not being read. At least I would have the joy of knowing that those lovely lucid eyes had rested on these pages.

I don't know if you read, at the time, some intelligent and too-indulgent articles on this book which will perhaps amuse you because they say something about your neighbour and even his bedroom (Lucien Daudet, M. Rostand, J. Blanche etc.).[18] Thank you for telling me that I am read by one of your friends at the 'Front'. Nothing can make me prouder. Please accept Madame my respectful and grateful regards.

MARCEL PROUST

12

Madame,

The *Nouvelle Revue Française* has published my excerpts in 2 Issues [of] June and July. If I send you 3 (2 issues of July) it is because alas I can only have copies which have been torn apart in order to glue pieces of them on proofs of the 2nd volume which was supposed to appear then, and which the 'aspera fata' prevented.[19] But the pieces cut out should not be the same in the two Issues. With the two, you will have a single complete one. And alas I will no doubt be obliged to ask you for them back later. But, naturally you will have the whole work in one volume! I will send it to you complete![20] – What I said to you about the real meaning of each part being conferred on them only by the following part, you can find an example of in the June Issue.—In *Swann*, one might be surprised that Swann should always be entrusting his wife to M. de Charlus, presumed to be her lover, or rather one might be surprised that the author should go to the trouble of publishing yet again after so many vaudevillians of the lowest sort that blindness of husbands (or of lovers). Yet in the June Issue you will see, since the 1st indication of M. de Charlus's vice appears there, that the reason why Swann knew he could entrust his wife to M. de Charlus was quite different! But I had not wanted to announce it in the 1st volume, preferring to resign myself to being very banal, so that one might come to know the character as in life where people reveal themselves only little by little. Starting with the 3rd volume moreover one will see that Swann has nevertheless been mistaken; M. de Charlus had had relations with only one woman, and it was precisely Odette.[21] – It pains me to think that you are ill and cloistered, I would so much like nephritis and neuritis to be no more than a bad memory that would not prevent you in any way from leading a pleasant life. But I think that your company is worth more than that of others, which is for you a reason (quite personal) for appreciating solitude. Please accept Madame my very respectful greetings.

MARCEL PROUST

13

Madame,

Forgive me for not having yet thanked you: it is I who have received marvellous roses described by you with 'fragrance imperishable'[22] but various which, in the evocations of the true poet that you are, cause the aroma, at every hour of the day, by turns, now to infiltrate the agatized chiaroscuro of the 'Interiors'[23] or now to expand within the fluent and diluted atmosphere of the gardens.

Only . . . I have been so ill these days (in my bed which I have not left and without having noisily opened or closed the carriage entrance as I have it seems been accused of doing) that I have not been able to write. Physically, it was impossible for me. Keep the Revues as long as you like. —. By an astonishing chance Gide, of whom we were speaking, and whom I have not seen for 20 years, came to see me *while* we were speaking of him in our letters. But I was not in a condition to receive him. Thank you again Madame for the marvellous pages flushed with a smell of roses. Your very respectful

MARCEL PROUST

The successor to the valet de chambre makes noise and that doesn't matter. But later he knocks with little tiny raps. And that is worse.

14

[autumn 1914?]

Madame,

I am quite unwell as I write but I thank you deeply for the letter that has brought me I assure you a vision more enduring than a bouquet and as colourful. One after another lovely verses written in all periods to the glory of autumn roses the autumn rose of d'Aubigné 'more exquisite than any other' (an autumn rose is more exquisite than any other), Verlaine's: 'Ah! When will the roses of September bloom again,' Gérard de Nerval's 'Rose with violet heart flower of Ste Gudule' next to his trellis 'where vine with rose unites,'[24] not to mention the innumerable 'mature roses' of two poetesses my great friends whom I no longer see alas now that I no longer get up Mme de Noailles and Mme de Régnier, I have assembled in my memory a bouquet of all the *written roses*. Now yours seemed to me worthy of being added to them, and your prose of residing as neighbour with their verse. Upon your roses at dusk I would place this epigraph by Pelléas:

'I am a Rose in the shadows.'[25]

Deign to accept Madame, this hasty and suffering expression of my respectful gratitude.

MARCEL PROUST

15

Madame,

May my book have given you as much pleasure as I have had
in reading your letter. Perhaps certain painful parts of it concerning the dawn, and also certain worldly scenes, are fairly
accurate.[26] But the descriptions in it hardly satisfy me.—I
am not familiar with any of the regions you mention to me.
But I have so often dreamed of them; and you, with your pic-
torial and sunlit words, have brought colour and light into my
closed room. Your health has improved you tell me, and your
life become more beautiful. I feel great joy over this. I cannot
say the same for myself. My solitude has become even more
profound, and I know nothing of the sun but what your letter
tells me. It has thus been a blessed messenger, and contrary
to the proverb, this single swallow has made for me an entire
spring. Allow me to thank you for it, Madame, with all my
heart, and asking you to remember me to the Doctor, to lay at
your feet my most respectful regards.

MARCEL PROUST

16

Madame,

Yesterday I was grieving most profoundly. After so many family and friends killed in the war, the dearest perhaps after M. Hahn (who is in Argonne but doing well) a person rare and delightful Bertrand de Fénelon has been killed.[27] I did not believe that God could add to my pain, when I was informed of yours. And I have so much fallen into the habit, without knowing you, of sympathizing with your sorrows and your joys, through the wall where I sense you invisible and present, that this news of the death of Monsieur your brother has acutely saddened me.[28] I always think of you a great deal, I will think of you even more since you are grieving. Alas I know that this sympathy is a small thing. When we are suffering, the only words that touch us are the words of those who have known the person we loved and who can recall him to us. I myself have only an experience of sadness that is already very old and almost uninterrupted. Please be so good as to remember me to the Doctor, would you also thank your son (whom I have never seen either!) and who it appears asks so kindly for news of me from my servant. If I knew of some plaything or some book that might please him, how happy I would be to send it to him. But you would have to direct me. I hope that his tenderness and that of the Doctor will help you bear your hard affliction and I ask you Madame to accept my sincerest regards.

MARCEL PROUST

Lucien Daudet who came to see me this evening gave me better news of J. Clary.

17

Madame,

I hope that you will not find me too indiscreet. I have had a great deal of noise these past few days and as I am not well, I am more sensitive to it. I have learned that the Doctor is leaving Paris the day after tomorrow and can imagine all that this implies for tomorrow concerning the 'nailing' of crates. Would it be possible either to nail the crates this evening, or else not to nail them tomorrow until starting at 4 or 5 o'clock in the afternoon (if my attack ends earlier I would hasten to let you know).

Or else if it is indispensable to nail them in the morning, to nail them in the part of your apartment that is above my kitchen, and not that which is above my bedroom. I call above my bedroom that which is also above the adjoining rooms, and even on the 4th since a noise so discontinuous, so 'notice-able' as blows being struck, is heard even in the areas where it is slightly diminished.[29] I confess that it bothers me very much to speak to you of such things and I am more embarrassed by it than I can say. My excuse for doing so today is perhaps first that I haven't done it at all this year; then that the circulars of the Minister of War follow one another so rapidly and so contradictorily that my military situation, already settled three times it seems is once again called into question. I await my visit from the Major announced ten days ago and which has not yet occurred, something that gives me only too many reasons to live 'keeping an ear out', interferes with my fumigations which might bother him (since I don't know the day or the hour of his coming) and thus leaving me more defenceless in the face of my ailments.[30] Following upon your trip, this situation has prevented me from repeating a visit that had left upon me such a charming impression. And your son is no longer here which saddens me also, for he at least could perhaps have 'come down' if I cannot 'go up' and I have with respect to him numerous debts which cry out to me about promises not kept. I don't know if you have seen Clary at the Hôtel d'Albe.[31] I have not been able to visit him yet and dread at the same time as I desire the emotion of such a moment.

Please accept Madame my very respectful greetings.

MARCEL PROUST

Don't tire yourself out answering me!

18

Madame,

I had ordered these flowers for you and I am in despair that they are coming on a day when against all expectation I feel so ill that I would like to ask you for silence tomorrow Saturday. Yet as this request is in no way conjoined with the flowers, causing them to lose all their fragrance as disinterested mark of respect and to bristle with nasty thorns, I would like even more not to ask you for this silence. If you are remaining as I am in Paris and if one evening I were not suffering too much, I would like since the Doctor and your son I believe have left and perhaps you are feeling a little lonely to come up sometime in the next few weeks to keep you company. But actually doing this encounters so many obstacles. I have three times in the evening and with what difficulty hired rather leisurely cars to go to see Clary, who Madame Rehbinder said was asking to see me.[32] The 1st time I went with Madame de la Béraudière to the rue du Colisée where we were told he no longer lived and was at 32 rue Gali ~~Colisée~~ lée.[33] At 32 rue Galilée the concierge got out of bed to tell us that he . . . did not know Clary. Madame Rehbinder corrected the mistake and told me that he lived at 33. I went off again another evening when I rang at number 33 a fantastic house with no Clary. Finally on the 3rd attempt I got it right with number 37. But then, I mistook the floor the elevator went up to the top causing me to do the opposite of what the Doctor's clients do each day ringing at my door. And when I went back down I felt [*word missing: that*] the

concierge would not let me go up again, swearing to me that Clary had gone to bed.[34]

Your very respectful and devoted

MARCEL PROUST

19

Madame,

Since you have been so good as to ask me, you permit me to tell you very frankly. Yesterday at about 7.30 a.m., today at about 8, 8.15 I was a little bothered and you will understand why. Having had yesterday (at last) the visit from the Major who deferred me for a few months,[35] I had promised myself to change my hours in order to be able to experience a little daylight. And to start with, not having slept for several days, I had granted myself four hours of sleep to quiet an attack. And at 10 o'clock in the morning I was supposed to get up. But at 8 o'clock, the light little knocks on the floorboards above me were so precise, that the veronal was useless and I woke, only too early for my attack to have been quieted.

[*Insertion of this little phrase below 'woke'*] This could have started before, I was asleep, I'm not saying that the loudest was at 8.15.

I had to give up my fine plans to change my hours, (which I will perhaps resume, but that does not depend on my will but on my health), take once again (since my attack is raging) medications upon medications, too much, which has made everything worse. —. I tell you this since you ask me because I know that you understand this, the regret for a reform of myself will wait for such a long time, prevented by such little noises (to which in a few days the reform had it been successful would no doubt have made me indifferent). What bothers me is never continuous noise, even loud noise, if it is not *struck*, on the floorboards, (it is less often no doubt in the bedroom itself, than at the bend of the hallway). And everything that is dragged over the floor, that falls on it, runs across it. —. It has been four days now that I have wanted to send you the vegetal reply to your Roses.[36] The wait for the Major prevented me from sending it. At last I will be able to. —. But I am disappointed: you had promised me you would ask me for some books, some illustrated ones, some Ruskin? It is perhaps heavy on your bed . . . How I would like to know Madame how you are. I think of you all the time. Please be so kind as to accept my respectful gratitude

MARCEL PROUST

[*Above the word 'Madame', on the first page*] What I do not express to you because I am suffering so today that I can't write, is my emotion, my gratitude for those letters you have written me, truly admirable and touching in mind and heart.

20

Madame,

I have been wanting for a long time to express to you my regret that the sudden arrival of my brother prevented me from writing to you during the last days of your stay in Paris, then my sadness at your leaving. But you have bequeathed to me so many workers and one Lady Terre[37] – whom I do not dare call, rather, 'Terrible' (since, when I get the workers to extend the afternoon a little in order to move things ahead without waking me too much, she commands them violently and perhaps sadistically to start banging at *7 o'clock in the morning* above my head, in the room immediately above my bedroom, an order which they are forced to obey), that I have no strength to write and have had to give up going away. How right I was to be discreet when you wanted me to investigate whether the morning noise was coming from a sink. What was that compared to those hammers? 'A shiver of water on moss' as Verlaine says of a song 'that weeps only to please you'.[38] In truth, I cannot be sure that the latter was hummed in order to please me. As they are redoing a shop next door I had with great difficulty got them not to begin work each day until after two o'clock. But this success has been destroyed since upstairs, much closer, they are beginning at 7 o'clock. I will add in order to be fair that your workers whom I do not have the honour of knowing (any more than the terrible lady) must be charming. Thus your painters (or your painter), unique within their kind and their guild, do not practise the Union of the Arts, do not sing! Generally a painter, a house painter especially, believes he must cultivate at the same time as the art of Giotto that of Reszke.[39] This one is quiet while the electrician bangs. I hope that when you return you will not find yourself surrounded by anything less than the Sistine frescoes ... I would so much like your voyage to do you good, I was so sad, so continually sad over your illness. If your charming son, innocent of the noise that is tormenting me, is with you, will you please convey all my best wishes to him and be so kind as to accept Madame my most respectful regards.

MARCEL PROUST

21

Madame,

I am extremely embarrassed that I have not yet thanked you. The real Truth is that I always defer letters (which could seem to ask you for something) to a moment when it is too late and when consequently, they are no longer indiscreet. Considering how little time it took to do the work on Ste Chapelle (this comparison can only I think be seen as flattering), one may presume that when this letter reaches Annecy, the beautifications of Boulevard Haussmann will be nearly done.

The real truth, I said, the 'Truth' as Pelléas says, is not to be found in the letter that was addressed to you, a fragment of which you wanted to communicate to me (I do not have it at hand, but will reproduce it for you). It is rather a dispatch from the Wolff Agency.[40] In any case I am not very well placed to judge on my own. I feel no resentment towards Madame *Terre* [earth] (one does say the *Sun* King and Madame *Mère* [mother]).[41] I have adapted for her, in honour of that Cybele who perhaps announces silence to the dead but not to the living, more than one piece of verse, beginning with the famous sonnet.

Alas I bear an evil whose name – well known – is Earth
This evil has no cure, and thus my lips are sealed
And she whom I lament knows nothing of my woe
Hereunder where I lie, I no doubt pass unseen,
Reposing at her feet and yet still quite alone,

And till the end I will have done my time on earth
Ne'er asking aught but stillness and receiving none.
She whom God has fashioned neither sweet nor kind,
Determined in her mind that I will have to hear
This ceaseless noise of hamm'ring now raiséd at her steps,
To holy Pity faithless every livelong day,
Will say when she shall read these lines so filled with her,
'Who can this woman be?' and will not comprehend.[42]

Besides, who knows? – I have always thought that noise would be bearable if it were continuous. As they are repairing the Boulevard Haussmann at night, redoing your apartment during the day and demolishing the shop at 98 bis in the intermissions, it is probable that when this harmonious team disperses, the silence will resound in my ears so abnormally that, mourning the vanished electricians and the departed carpet-layer, I will miss my Lullaby. Deign to accept Madame my respectful greetings.

MARCEL PROUST

22

[November 1915?]

Madame,

As Annecy was for me voiceless (if the Boulevard Haussmann was not noiseless), I do not know if you received my latest letters and especially those in which I passed on to you the respects of poor Clary.[43] —. This one is just a quick note from a neighbour. I am forced to go out very ill and do not know in what state I will return! Yet tomorrow is Sunday, a day which usually offers me the opposite of the weekly repose because in the little courtyard adjoining my room they beat the carpets from your apartment, with an extreme violence. May I ask for grace *tomorrow*? Or when I do my fumigation let them know so that they can take advantage of that time. I hope that you will not find me too indiscreet and I lay at your feet my respectful regards.

MARCEL PROUST

Mme Williams and her harp.

23

Madame,

Your letter fills me with gratitude (and sadness since you seem to believe there could be doubts on my part). The epistolary 'silence' for which it is too good of you to apologize had been accompanied by another silence which I perceived very distinctly for the past six days and which it was sweet for me to owe to you. The sweetness of your presence and your intention was incarnate in it, and I savoured it with thankfulness. I fear that the unexpected arrival this evening at midnight of my friend Reynaldo Hahn who for the 1st time in 15 months was returning from the front and who entered in disarray may have occasioned some noise which would so ill have recompensed that which you are sparing me.[44] I was very moved to see him again. I do not know to what extent my health will allow me to see him during the 6 days that he will be spending in Paris but I will ask him not to be so noisy again. He comes up like a whirlwind and goes down in the same way, I can't understand that. Alas he will not be coming back again until the end of the war ... —. I also wonder if the voice of my housekeeper, very sharp, does not rise to you. She stays with me very late and does not make any noise when she moves about. But if her voice could be heard, I implore you to tell me. In prescribing for me certain modifications in my ways of doing things, I cannot express to you the intimate pleasure that you would give me. Their daily repetition would mingle your image with my obedience. 'Nothing is so sweet as her authority.'[45] I am a little sorry that you have not received my last letters (though they were addressed I believe quite correctly). The pastiche of Thérésa's Song: 'This is the earth [*terre*]!' would have made you smile, I believe and was less bad than that of the sonnet of Arvers which you did receive, I think.[46] Clary told me what a great musician you were. Will I never be able to come up and hear you? The Franck quartet, the *Béatitudes*, the Beethoven Quartets (all music that I have in fact here) are the objects of my most nostalgic desire.[47] I have never once been well enough to go to hear them (last Sunday the *Béatitudes* was performed, but I was wheezing in my bed) and when by chance a musician comes to see me in the evening, I stop him from making music for me so that the noise may not bother you. What compensation if on one of the very rare evenings when I can get up, you should permit me to hear you. Thank you again Madame and please accept my lively and grateful respects.

MARCEL PROUST

24

[December 19, 1916]
Tuesday 10 o'clock – evening

Madame,

Alas upon returning home in the grip of the most violent attack I find your charming letter. The letter offers me the most delicious pleasure, the attack pitilessly denies me it. When it has subsided a little tomorrow, if it subsides, I will go to bed and will not be able to get up again for *several days*, what a stupid idea I had to go out for a moment today. If I had stayed in bed, I could have got up tomorrow, spent the afternoon with you, gone to shake the hand of my old and dear Maître France who in the past first introduced me to the public.[48] He remembers me and forgives me I am told by Lucien Daudet who sees him often. I was determined not to go out tomorrow, I had told Montesquiou I would not go to hear Madame Rubinstein pronounce some wounded offerings, and it was because I was so determined not to go out tomorrow that I made this stupid outing today, with no interest, with none of the pleasure that I would have had tomorrow.[49] So I am disappointed and disheartened. —. Ever since the day on which you brought me the bright interval of your visit I have been ill the whole time. What is more the Strauses, whom I left that day, may have told you that I have not been able to see them since, for I know that you are close to them. And I have not been able to see Clary either. On the other hand I have had the joy of often having by my bedside my brother who after having been very unwell is in Paris for a little while. I wanted to mention to him the name of your mutual friend of whom you had spoken to me and have not been [*word missing: able*] to recall it. Happily your letters are too remarkable for one not to keep them. And I will thus find the name again. What will happen, at the theatre, to those admirable phrases of *S. Bonnard* which I know by heart and which my memory though so enfeebled will retain until the end like a piece of music one has loved as a child. What a joy it would have been to bring together the susceptibilities of our memories and the exigencies of our predilection to listen to that.[50] Perhaps it's just as well. At the theatre *Crainquebille* made me weep.[51] I envy you Madame that tomorrow among the 'acta Sanctorum' of the Learned Bollandistes you will see old Sylvestre Bonnard, and I thank you for having had the thought of inducing me to see it, as Bonnard, (the very old Bonnard that I am) would have thanked the Countess Trépof for the precious legend.

Please be so kind as to remember me to the Doctor and accept Madame my most grateful regards

MARCEL PROUST

25

Madame,

I ask your permission to keep, today as well – in order to ennoble this tragic Christmas which does not bring 'Peace on earth to men of good will' – the wonderful and moving images which will be restored to you tomorrow.[52] And really through this miraculous vision you have, with a disconcertingly inventive intelligence, continued beyond what is possible what we were saying the other day about the Countess Trépof in *Sylvestre Bonnard*.[53] Because in fact it is in the form of a Yule log that the incomparable *Lives of the Saints* has come to me, the amazing *Golden Legend*, or rather purplish (for a compatriot of Doctor Williams told me the other day that Reims, for its sublime steeple alas, has turned the most extraordinary *purple*)[54] the Bible of Reims which is no longer intact like the Bible of Amiens, the stones of Reims which fulfil the prophecy: 'And the very stones shall cry out to demand justice.' Perhaps, moreover, the disaster of Reims, a thousand times more pernicious for humanity than that of Louvain – and for Germany first of all, for whom Reims, because of Bamberg, was the favourite cathedral – was a crime rather coldly conceived. War is war and we are not only lamenting a humanity of stones. But that of Reims whose smile seemed to herald that of da Vinci, in its draperies which are bewilderingly reminiscent of the most beautiful period of Greece was unique. Neither Amiens though more austerely biblical, nor Chartres though more sacredly immaterial were that. And no doubt I know very well that many deplore Reims who have never lifted their eyes to Notre Dame and who naively believe that the most beautiful church in Paris is our parish church, our ugly Saint Augustin. But I who insofar as my health permits make to the stones of Reims pilgrimages as piously awestruck as to the stones of Venice believe I am justified in speaking of the diminution to humanity that will be consummated on the day when the arches that are already half burnt away collapse forever on those angels who without troubling themselves about the danger still gather marvellous fruits from the lush stylized foliage of the forest of stones. My too ailing eyes which refuse to serve me this evening interrupt a prattle that would be interminable for can one be brief when one sees torn to shreds on France what Saint Bernard I believe (but I believe I'm wrong about the author) called the white mantle of churches.[55] I will send back to you tomorrow the Holy Images, the immortal wounded, and I thank you today for your thought with most grateful respect.

MARCEL PROUST

26

Madame,

I am abashed (and delighted!) that you have written to me. You're right in thinking that it wasn't a matter of 'sending flowers'. But a woman who has unique greenhouses having given me these two carnations which seemed to me truly rare, I sent them to you, after having hesitated between you, Helleu, and Jacques Blanche, that is to say, between three lovers of refined colours to whom one sends a flower as one would send a butterfly wing. I am glad about what you tell me concerning the imminent arrival of your son. I am glad above all for you. But also a little selfishly for myself as I would very much like to see mother and son. And to see the son would perhaps be less difficult. For an ill person feels, even so, his vanity less embarrassed in allowing all the sad apparatus of his illness to be seen by a child, even a charming one, than by a woman. Since you speak to me about my health, I ask your help for Sunday morning. Monday would be more logical since it is on Sunday that I must go to see friends and therefore Monday that I will be ill. But my request is on the contrary for Sunday. Because if on Sunday morning there is too much noise I will not be able to get up in the afternoon. —. I still have not been able to see Clary again and it grieves me very much. What fate that here in Paris where it is almost impossible to find one apartment near another, mother and son succeeded, perhaps by chance, in finding themselves adjacent, Madame Clary having only to knock on her kitchen wall for her son to hear her, and that she should have died without their seeing each other again. Already I carry around with me in my mind so many dissolved deaths, that each new one causes supersaturation and crystallizes all my griefs into an infrangible block. Most respectfully your grateful

MARCEL PROUST

Translator's afterword

As we read these letters, it is helpful to picture the room in which Proust wrote them, and him in the room. Although one would imagine that the room would be preserved as a museum, even furnished with Proust's own furniture (which is extant), that is not the case. Proud though the French are of one of their premier authors, the apartment at 102 Boulevard Haussmann in which he lived for nearly twelve years and in which he wrote most of *In Search of Lost Time* is now part of the premises of a bank. Some years ago – I don't know if this is still the case – it was, at least, possible to visit the room during the summer by appointment on Thursday afternoons. One was shown around by a bank employee, with interruptions when she had to go off and answer a banking question.

Proust's bedroom was unpopulated for much of the day, unless it was being used for a meeting with a client or among bank officials. A portrait of Proust hung on the wall, but the talk in the room would have been about financial matters, and though financial matters interested the generous, extravagant, impulsive Proust – see the passage in letter 9 in which he tells Mme Williams that he was (several months before the start of WWI) 'more or less completely ruined' – his spirit would probably not be present. It might drift in for a moment if those taking part in the meeting paused to recall him and his life and work. And French bankers and their clients would conceivably have a strong interest in and respect for Proust.

The room gave the impression of being rather small, perhaps because of its very high ceiling, which Proust's housekeeper estimated to be some fourteen feet high. Yet Proust described it as 'vast' when he made the difficult decision to rent the apartment, and in fact the room measured nine and a half paces by six, as a visitor without measuring tape might estimate it, which translates as roughly six and a half metres by four and a half, or over twenty-nine square metres. Maybe it seemed small because it was so relatively empty, containing only a sideboard, a bookcase, a small table in the centre, and four small chairs.

According to the bank employee-cum-guide, certain structural parts of the room were the same as they had been in Proust's time: the two tall windows; two of the four doors; the mouldings around the tops of the walls; the parquet floor; and the fireplace with its thick white marble mantel. There were few outward signs that this room had anything to do with Proust: in addition to the portrait on the wall, there was a short row of volumes of the Proust Society's quarterly journal occupying part of one shelf in the otherwise empty glass-fronted bookcase, one that had not belonged to Proust; and, on the top of the sideboard, which also had not belonged to Proust, a small sign announcing 'Proust's bedroom' alongside a stack of brochures about the actual Proust Museum, which was elsewhere – in the house of 'Tante Léonie' out in Illiers-Combray, one and a half hours from the city.

When Proust lived in it, when he rested, slept, ate, wrote,

read, inhaled his smoking Legras powders, drank his coffee, and entertained visitors there, it was crowded with furniture. We learn from a description by his housekeeper and faithful companion Céleste that there was, for instance, a large wardrobe between the two windows, and, in front of the wardrobe, so close that its doors could not be opened, a grand piano. Between the grand piano and the bed, an armchair as well as the three small tables which Proust used for three different purposes. Other pieces of furniture – a bookcase, a work table that had belonged to Proust's mother, a different sideboard – stood at various spots against the walls. Céleste had to squeeze her way in and out.

My guide pointed out the corner in which Proust's bed had been placed, along the wall opposite the windows, and where he wrote a great deal of the novel. Standing between the head of the bed and the wall, an Oriental screen protected him from draughts and helped buffer him from the noise that came from the adjoining building, on the other side of the wall.

Noise from construction within the building or from next door was a continuing menace and plague for Proust during his years here, as we can see from the letters in the present collection. It was the neighbour on the *entresol* below, one Dr Gagey, who was having work done on his apartment when Proust first moved in, in the last days of 1906, as we know from the complaints, sometimes humorous, in his other, voluminous letters. Just as the work on Dr Gagey's apartment was ending and relief for Proust was in sight, work began in the building next door, where one Mme Katz was installing a new bathroom just a few feet from his head. (Kafka, at about this time, was recording the same sorts of complaints in his diaries, though he liked to turn them into small stories about what fantastic things these neighbours might be doing.)

After the death of his mother, Proust had made the decision not to continue living in the too-large, memory-haunted family apartment. This apartment at 102 Boulevard Haussmann was just one possible choice of residence among many which Proust had investigated by proxy, with the help of a host of friends and without moving from his temporary rooms in a hotel at Versailles. It is therefore surprising to realize that he was in fact a quarter-owner of the building at the time, his brother owning another quarter and his aunt the other half.

When he moved in, he considered the apartment to be no more than a transitional residence. It was the first he had ever lived in on his own, but it was a familiar part of his past: his mother had known it well, and his uncle had lived and died here – Proust had in fact visited him on his deathbed, in the same room that became his bedroom. He later, through inattention, and without fully realizing the consequences, allowed his aunt to buy his own share and his brother's, and thus had no say in the matter when she in turn decided, in 1919, to sell the building to a banker, who intended to convert the premises into a bank, obliging him to move, against his will, and in fact twice more. This was only three years before his death, and in Céleste's opinion hastened his decline.

In order to talk about the context of the letters in this volume – including the room in which Proust wrote them and the apartment in which the room was situated – it is helpful to have some sense of the geography of Proust's building. The French system of numbering is the same as the British: what the French call the first floor is the floor above the ground floor, the second floor is two floors above street level, etc. Proust's apartment was on the first floor, the dentist's practice on the second, the dentist's apartment on the third. But, complicating this numbering system, in the case of Proust's building, was the *entresol*, that low-ceilinged half-floor which can be between any two floors but is generally between the ground floor and the first, in which case we in English call it the mezzanine.

When there is an *entresol*, the floor above it may in fact be called the second floor, and this is what Proust calls it at least once in this collection of letters, as do the editors of the French edition. Other sources, including the memoir of his housekeeper Céleste, call it the first. (There is no disagreement about where Proust lived, just some inconsistency about how to number the floor.) We will adhere to the traditional French system in discussing the apartments and inhabitants of 102 Boulevard Haussmann.

However, to clarify matters: there was, at that address, first the ground floor, which in those days was entered through a two-panelled carriage entrance (the same that Proust mentions indignantly in letter 13). This level contained, at least, an apartment occupied by the concierge Antoine and his family. One flight up, there was the *entresol*, under Proust's apartment, occupied by Dr Gagey, his wife, and their daughter. Another flight up was Proust's apartment. Above it was the practice of the American dentist Charles Williams, on the street side directly above Proust's head, as well as, in the back, his laboratory. Since this latter workplace was located away from the street, looking out on the courtyard, Proust was not bothered by the footsteps of the several assistants who worked there.

Above Dr Williams's practice was the apartment occupied by the Williamses and their small son, who was about four years old when they moved in. There were another two floors above the Williamses' apartment, but it is not clear who lived in them, though on the top floor, under the roof, there would usually have been small independent rooms connected by a narrow corridor, the bedrooms of the servants who worked in the apartments below. There was a back stairway which Proust referred to as the service stairs or 'small' stairs. This was used by the building's servants, and by the concierge when he brought up a message for Proust, discreetly tapping at the kitchen door to avoid the disturbance of ringing the doorbell, and for other deliveries, including the milk, brought daily by the neighbourhood *crémerie* for Proust's coffee. Somewhere in Proust's apartment, probably near or next to the kitchen – though it is not clear from the simplified floor plan of the apartment included in this volume exactly where – was a bedroom for the use of a servant, and this was where Céleste slept after she moved in sometime in 1914.

There have of course been changes in the layout of the rooms since the time Proust lived here. There is now a door at the head of Proust's bed. The corridor outside his bedroom, across which he used to step on the way to his dressing room and bath, now extends into the building next door. The other door out of his bedroom, the door he assigned to be used by visitors and by his housekeeper, opens into a generous room with a massive conference table in the centre and a fireplace at either end. Here too, very little is original: the fireplaces, the wood floor, and the windows. But a change in the wood of the parquet floor marks the line where a wall stood, separating Proust's large drawing room from a small anteroom where his guests used to wait to see him.

These three rooms line the street side of the apartment. To the rear of them, towards the courtyard, there are other vestiges: the marble surface of the stairs and landing by which visitors approached the apartment; the shaft for the small elevator (though it is a different elevator) that rises up in the centre of the stairwell; the oeil-de-boeuf window through which Céleste used to look out into the stairwell to see who was coming up. Proust's visitors stopped and waited on the landing in front of the front door to the apartment, but there is no longer a wall or a door there, only open space and two white pillars. Nowadays, from a spot that was once inside the apartment, you can watch the stairwell as men in shirtsleeves and ties, carrying folders, walk up from the landing that would have opened into the apartment of Dr Gagey, and on up to the next floor – the floor where Dr Williams had his practice and his laboratory of assistants – or come trotting back down, talking finance. Visitors now coming up to the first floor to do business with the bank will see, when they walk into what used to be Proust's apartment (across what used to be the entryway, where his gloves and handkerchiefs sat in a silver salver), an open area with a sofa and armchairs, and they may sit there to talk. This was in fact Proust's dining room, though the walls are gone and he used it not as a dining room but as a storeroom. He had inherited a great deal of the contents of the family apartment, and did not want to part with much of it, but could not find places for it all in the other rooms, so he filled the dining room until it was 'like a forest', according to Céleste. An imaginative financier with a little information might be haunted, sitting next to the lone potted plant, by the lingering presence of a crowded accumulation of heavy fin de siècle furniture and bric-a-brac.

There is no balcony on the front of the building now, though Proust describes stepping out onto the balcony from his bedroom and actually enjoying a rare contact with sunlight. The apartment is no longer a set of rooms whose closed shutters and curtains create an eternal night, but is now glowingly well lit, with its high ceilings and tall windows, prosperous and busy.

A fourth reference to Proust in his former bedroom is not immediately obvious: the walls are lined with cork. But this is a marbleized, decorative cork that has been put on the walls since Proust's time, and it is not even obviously cork unless you look closely. It is a sort of compromise cork, a stand-in for Proust's cork. In Proust's time, the bank officer explains, the walls were crudely lined with thick slabs of raw bark off the cork trees that grow in the south of France, painted over in black so as to protect Proust's lungs from the material's crumbling or disintegration – though Proust's servant has described the cork as being the colour of honey. The famous cork was suggested to Proust's close friend Anna de Noailles, a poet and another noise-phobic, who used it in her own home.

The extant contents of Proust's bedroom are in the Musée Carnavalet, the city museum of Paris. They are down a corridor and within hailing distance of the recreated bedroom of Anna de Noailles. Here, too, square tiles of cork line the walls of Proust's room, a plain tan cork which the literature of the museum describes as an exact replica of Proust's cork. In Illiers-Combray, there are a few more objects from Proust's apartment: the dishes he ate from; the coffee maker used by Céleste to make his special coffee; several shelves of books.

Because they are the real thing and not approximations, Proust's bedroom furniture – the brass bedstead, the bedside table and lamp, the desk, the sideboard, the chaise longue, two armchairs, and the Oriental screen – are haunted by his presence, especially those with signs of wear: most of all, because so intimately associated with the human body, the places on the upholstery where the nap of the fabric has been worn down to the thread, not only by Proust but by others, too, presumably his mother, his father, his brother, and his visiting friends.

Because of his illness, Proust spent most of his time in bed, heavily dressed in – according to one account – two sweaters, socks, and long underwear, with a hot-water bottle at his feet that was renewed three times a day. A blanket folded in four hung over the large door to the room to protect him from draughts and noise. Both shutters and curtains were closed over the double-paned windows, so that no sound could be heard from the street. The chandelier that hung from the ceiling was never illuminated. A candle was kept burning, since he lit his powders using a folded paper rather than striking a match. He generally woke 'for the day' at nine in the evening, and had his only meal at that time – coffee and a croissant which Céleste would bring to him when he rang.

When he felt well enough, Proust liked to have a friend visit occasionally, as long as that friend followed certain rules: no cigarettes, of course, no perfume. Proust describes Reynaldo Hahn coming in, playing the piano for a little while, and then leaving again 'like a hurricane' (or, at other times, 'like a whirlwind' – as Proust puts it apologetically in letter 23).

One can pause to listen, via YouTube, to the composition by Reynaldo Hahn mentioned in the note to letter 23, *Le ruban dénoué* [The untied ribbon], twelve waltzes for two pianos. As performed by two Italian pianists in a lamplit chamber concert in Rome, it is at times dynamic and forceful, more often gentle. The audience, visible in the background, is so absolutely still that for a while you might think the video has been manipulated and they have been frozen visually. From this, you may stray over to Anne Sofie von Otter singing another composition of Hahn's, a three-minute song. Her voice is liquid, effortless. In contrast to his style of entering and leaving Proust's building, Hahn's compositions tend to be calm, balanced and elegant, intimate, moderate in tempos and dynamics, and characterized by uncluttered simplicity, charm, and sentimentality. Hahn himself, though a singer and gifted interpreter of his music, apparently smoked and talked too much.

Many friends have described visiting Proust in the room, among them the writer Maurice Rostand, who says of the room: 'Everything was left lying around, his aspirins and his dress shoes; books were piled up in pyramids; ties were strewn alongside catalogues, invitation cards to the British embassy lay next to medical prescriptions . . .'

Céleste herself, in her memoir, remembers that the predominant colour was blue, and the lamp next to his bed cast a green light because of the shade. She describes the room as perpetually dark as night, and densely smoke-filled when Proust had been burning his powders. The smoke from these powders would sometimes drift under the doors and out into the rest of the building, and the neighbours would sometimes complain.

And it has to be said that in other ways, too, Proust was in his own turn guilty, on occasion, of disturbing his neighbours. He describes to a different correspondent how another long-time close friend, Robert de Montesquiou, came by in the early hours of the morning and, in his emotion, kept stamping on the floor 'without pity' for the Gagey family sleeping downstairs (whom Céleste in her memoir describes as *plutôt des couches-tôt*, or 'rather early-to-bedders').

Or, several times, Proust, a great lover of music, and not well enough to go out to concerts very often, would hire musicians to come and play for him in his bedroom. Once, at 1 a.m., impulsively and without prior warning, he sent for the Poulet Quartet to come and play César Franck's quartet.

Before beginning, the musicians (in the room lit only by candles) hung cloths over the opening of the fireplace to stop the sound from travelling – though one would think that was hardly effectual. When they reached the end of the piece, at two in the morning, Proust induced them (for a handsome sum) to start over and play the whole piece again.

But Proust was well liked by his neighbours, on the whole, for the same qualities so evident in his letters to Mme Williams: his grace, eloquence, thoughtfulness, sympathy, gestures of gratitude. Evidence of these good relations is not hard to find: an inscription in a copy of his Ruskin translation, *La Bible d'Amiens*, to his 'good neighbour', one Arthur Pernolet, who occupied the apartment above him before the arrival of Dr Williams, and whom Proust knew already before he moved in; the helpfulness of Mme Gagey when the time came for most (or all?) of the tenants of the building to move out – she supplied Proust with the results of her own research into suitable apartments; and the fact that a year after they were no longer neighbours, having scattered to other buildings, Dr Gagey came to Proust in answer to a request for a consultation: oddly enough – perfectly symbolic – he had put something in his ear to block the ambient noise, it had got stuck, and the ear was infected.

As the vast resources of the Internet allow us to walk along a Paris street that is almost unchanged from the 1920s and gaze up at – or even float over – the building in which one of Proust's friends died, and as it allows us within a few seconds to begin listening to one of Reynaldo Hahn's compositions, or to leaf through the caricatures of the very popular singer Thérésa, with whom Hahn was infatuated, so it also reveals more of the life of Proust's building: the wartime activities of Proust's downstairs neighbour, the *couche-tôt* Dr Gagey, who was commended in 1915 for his ambulance service 'in circumstances often difficult and always perilous'; and the legacies of the former upstairs neighbour, Proust's friend Pernolet, who, after his death, also in 1915, left funds to at least two Paris museums for the acquisition of paintings. Follow every reference in these letters, and Proust's world opens out before us.

Proust, so very solitary, as he says in many of his letters, and devoting most of his waking hours to his work, was also intensely gregarious and an uninhibited talker. When he was feeling well enough, he talked without pause, and the person he talked to the most, because she was always available, was Céleste, an intelligent and responsive listener. He often rang for her after she had gone to bed, and she would come as she was, in her nightgown and robe, her hair 'down her back', as she says. He would talk to her for hours at a time, sitting up in bed leaning against two pillows, while she stood at the foot of the bed.

Gide describes, in his journal, Proust's style of talking: 'His conversation, ceaselessly cut by parenthetical clauses, runs on . . .'

The diplomat and Proust fan Paul Morand enlarges upon this: the Proustian sentence was 'singsong, cavilling, reasoned, answering objections the listener would never have thought of making, raising unforeseen difficulties, subtle in its shifts and pettifoggery, stunning in its parentheses – that, like helium balloons, held the sentence aloft – vertiginous in its length . . . well constructed despite its apparent disjointedness; . . . you listened spellbound . . .'

This style, so natural to him in conversation, pours out also in his letters – letters, as his friend Robert Dreyfus put it, 'in which he always wanted to say everything, as in his books, and in which he succeeded by means of an infinity of parentheses, sinuosities, and reversals'. It is the same style that is evident, though more strictly controlled, in the extended, balanced periodic sentences of his finished, published work (or, perhaps one should say, never quite finished, but brought to a certain point and then ended). Here is an example from letter 23, with Proust's characteristic paucity of punctuation and his multiple enclosed subordinate clauses: 'My friend Reynaldo Hahn who for the 1st time in 15 months was returning from the front and who entered in disarray may have occasioned some noise which would so ill have recompensed that which you are sparing me . . .'

Another example of the spare punctuation can be seen in letter 14: 'I am quite unwell as I write but I thank you deeply for the letter that has brought me I assure you a vision more enduring than a bouquet and as colourful.' And, later in the same letter: '. . . not to mention the innumerable "mature roses" of two poetesses my great friends whom I no longer see alas now that I no longer get up Mme de Noailles and Mme de Régnier' – note the interpolated comment and at least five, by my count, commas missing which would be present in a more standard syntax.

We are told that Proust wrote very fast. This, too, is apparent in the letters, in the sprawling handwriting, in the tendency to abbreviate, in the occasional missing word, and perhaps, though not necessarily, in the missing punctuation.

Yet, at the same time, his syntactical agility is always in evidence, as in letter 13, in which he includes in one fairly short sentence a rather elaborate, and in this case indignant, parenthetical remark ('as I have been accused') that manages to enclose within it yet another clause ('it seems'): 'I have been so ill these days (in my bed which I have not left and without having noisily opened or closed the carriage entrance as I have it seems been accused of doing) that I have not been able to write.' Here he exemplifies, in a rougher, more urgent way, his declaration concerning his published writing that a sentence contains a complete thought, and that no matter how complex it may be, this thought should remain intact. The shape of the sentence is the shape of the thought, and every word is necessary.

Perhaps the most extreme example, in this collection of letters, of his complex syntax, and lack of punctuation, as well as his colourful and fertile imagination, comes in letter 25, which is mainly devoted to the cathedral of Reims so heavily damaged by bombardment in the first autumn of the war. Here we approach the precision, the rhetorical heights, and the luscious imagery of *In Search of Lost Time* (and with a reference to a Ruskin title covertly slipped in): 'But I who insofar as my health permits make to the stones of Reims pilgrimages as piously awestruck as to the stones of Venice believe I am justified in speaking of the diminution to humanity that will be consummated on the day when the arches that are already half burnt away collapse forever on those angels who without troubling themselves about the danger still gather marvellous fruits from the lush stylized foliage of the forest of stones.'

The acute understanding of psychology and social behaviour displayed so richly in the novel is another continuing thread in the letters, and is especially apparent in letter 21: 'I always defer letters (which could seem to ask you for something) to a moment when it is too late and when consequently, they are no longer indiscreet.'

And the gentle touches of humour, so prevalent in the novel, also have their place in the letters, as in the continuation of letter 21: 'Considering how little time it took to do the work on Ste Chapelle (this comparison can only I think be seen as flattering), one may presume that when this letter reaches Annecy, the beautifications of Boulevard Haussmann will be nearly done.' (With, later in the same letter, his comparison of the various noises that surround him to his Lullaby.)

How revealing letters can be, in the era when they were written by hand and rarely copied over, especially not by the suffering Proust, who so often, according to him, had barely the strength or energy to write even a short note. Unrevised, a letter may show the thread of the thought as it develops: 'When it has subsided,' Proust writes, of one of his attacks, in letter 24, and then realizes it may not subside, and so goes on to add what has just occurred to him: 'if it subsides.'

The letters, written over a span of years and in different moods and physical conditions, show different aspects of his personality and character. He may be gracious and flattering,

as in letter 11: 'At least I would have the joy of knowing that those lovely lucid eyes had rested on these pages'; or flowery and eloquent, as in letter 15: 'My solitude has become even more profound, and I know nothing of the sun but what your letter tells me. It has thus been a blessed messenger, and contrary to the proverb, this single swallow has made for me an entire spring.' Or, in contrast to his poetic descriptions, he may suddenly deploy, with cool adeptness, in letter 26, a metaphor taken from the world of chemistry: 'Already I carry around with me in my mind so many dissolved deaths, that each new one causes supersaturation and crystallizes all my griefs into an infrangible block.'

He is meticulous and particular not only in his requests as to when and where his upstairs neighbours might nail shut their crates, in letter 17: 'Or else if it is indispensable to nail them in the morning, to nail them in the part of your apartment that is above my kitchen, and not that which is above my bedroom. I call above my bedroom that which is also above the adjoining rooms, and even on the 4th'; but also in describing the nature itself of disturbance from noise (as he continues the sentence): '. . . since a noise so discontinuous, so "noticeable" as blows being struck, is heard even in the areas where it is slightly diminished.'

And in letter 19, too, he goes into detail about the effect of noise: 'What bothers me is never continuous noise, even loud noise, if it is not *struck*, on the floorboards, (it is less often no doubt in the bedroom itself, than at the bend of the hallway). And everything that is dragged over the floor, that falls on it, runs across it.' I think we readers, peering over

Mme Williams's shoulder, may find his precision amusing, but he himself, though so likely at other times to see the humour in a situation, here seems in deadly earnest. And the same earnestness must be present in another letter, letter 22, as he describes one of his weekly torments (again, with a somewhat eccentric placement or omission of commas): 'Yet tomorrow is Sunday, a day which usually offers me the opposite of the weekly repose because in the little courtyard adjoining my room they beat the carpets from your apartment, with an extreme violence.'

Proust's style, in these letters, then, is a mix of elegance and haste, refinement and convolution, gravity and self-mockery, marked by abbreviations and mistakes, very little punctuation, and no paragraphing to speak of, or almost none, as he shifts from topic to topic.

My approach to translating this style has been to hew very close to it, not supplying missing punctuation or correcting mistakes, but at the same time trying to retain as much of its grace, beauty, sudden shifts of tone and subject, and distinctive character as I could. It was a pleasurable challenge to attempt to reproduce his non sequiturs, his flowery constructions, his literary references, and his meticulous instructions for lessening the intrusions of noise. One is bound to feel compassion – as his neighbours did – for the beleaguered Proust, pushing ahead, against all odds and in the worst of health, with his vast project; it is certainly impossible, in any case, for anyone with neighbours to blame him for being so fussy about their noise.

One particular challenge in the translation was to create a passable version of Proust's pastiche in letter 21, of the sonnet by Félix Arvers. This poem became so famous in its day that Arvers has been dubbed a 'one-poem poet', so famous that it inspired a contemporary American poet to translate it. One would not immediately associate Henry Wadsworth Longfellow with Proust, and yet, for a time – not at the same time – they were both concentrating their attention, and their literary abilities, on 'My Secret'. We may gain yet another idea of the original from reading Longfellow's version, from which I had hoped to steal some phrases but managed only to take the last line:

My Secret

My soul its secret hath, my life too hath its mystery,
A love eternal in a moment's space conceived;
Hopeless the evil is, I have not told its history,
And she who was the cause nor knew it nor believed.

Alas! I shall have passed close by her unperceived,
Forever at her side, and yet forever lonely,
I shall unto the end have made life's journey, only
Daring to ask for naught, and having naught received.

For her, though God hath made her gentle and endearing,
She will go on her way distraught and without hearing
These murmurings of love that round her steps ascend,

Piously faithful still unto her austere duty,
Will say, when she shall read these lines full of her beauty,
'Who can this woman be?' and will not comprehend.

As for the other apparatus in the book, I have made only a few slight changes to the very helpful notes by Estelle Gaudry and Jean-Yves Tadié, and to M. Tadié's foreword, when it was necessary to supply a first name, for instance, or an identification, or otherwise enlarge upon a reference that might not be obvious to an Anglophone reader.

By way of coda: After these letters were brought into public view from where they had been residing in the Musée des Lettres et Manuscrits in Paris, and after some excerpts from them, in the original French, were published in *Le Nouvel Observateur* online, on October 10, 2013, an interesting response added a few more details to our understanding of Proust's life and activities.

A person by the lyrical name of Lerossignol – 'the nightingale' – writes an online comment to the article. He is the grandson of a florist with a shop in the seaside town of Houlgate, on the stretch of the Normandy coast aptly known as the Côte Fleurie (the Flowery Coast); Houlgate was a neighbouring town to Cabourg, where Proust liked to stay at the Grand Hôtel. Guests marvelled, according to Philippe Soupault in his memoirs, over 'how Monsieur Proust rented five expensive rooms, one to live in, the other four to "contain" the silence'. Cabourg became Balbec in Proust's novel. The flower shop was the one Proust patronized in the years 1908 to 1913 when sending flowers to, among others, Mme Williams. M. Lerossignol writes that the family archives in his possession include records of the shop's transactions which mention Proust's sending flowers to the Williamses;

he has therefore known the name for a long time and was aware that the couple must have been acquaintances of Proust's. But only now, with the publication of the present letters, does he know who they were. He would like, incidentally, to correct one statement in the commentary that accompanies the extracts – that in those days etiquette required that a man send flowers not directly to a married woman but to her husband. He can attest from his family records that this was not always the case, and he knows in which cases Proust sent flowers to the husband and in which, in fact, directly to the wife. With regard to the Williamses, however, he adds, Proust was always very correct. (See, for example, letter 3.) M. Lerossignol goes on to remark that Proust, despite his illness, did venture into the family flower shop: Lerossignol's grandmother counted thirty-two visits before 1912.

From the invoices of Proust's orders it is possible to know the names of those with whom Proust associated while staying at the vast Grand Hôtel Cabourg, before his health worsened to such an extent that he confined himself permanently to Paris. M. Lerossignol has had the idea of organizing a tour of the still surviving villas of those to whom Proust sent flowers in Houlgate ordered from Au Jardin des Roses, the florist of M. Lerossignol's grandparents, who were also named Lerossignol.

LYDIA DAVIS

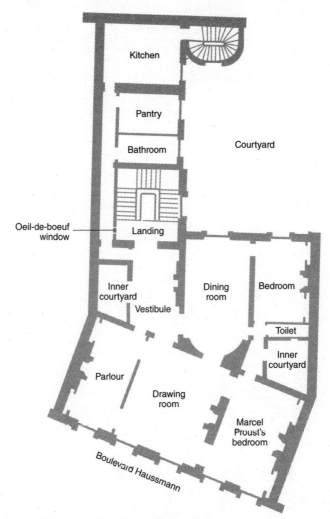

Kitchen

Pantry

Bathroom

Courtyard

Oeil-de-boeuf window

Landing

Inner courtyard

Vestibule

Dining room

Bedroom

Toilet

Inner courtyard

Parlour

Drawing room

Marcel Proust's bedroom

Boulevard Haussmann

Floor plan of the apartment in which Marcel Proust
lived from 1907 to 1919, at 102 Boulevard Haussmann.

Notes

[Content in brackets has been supplied by the translator.]

1. Céleste Albaret, *Monsieur Proust*, trans. Barbara Bray (Paris: Éditions Robert Laffont, 1973), p. 382. On Mme Straus, a client of Doctor Williams who considered him the best dentist in Paris and insisted on Proust's consulting him, see p. 108. See also note 4 below.

2. The line is from Victor Hugo's poem 'Ce que dit la bouche d'ombre' [What speaks the shadow's mouth] in his collection *Les Contemplations* [Contemplations], published in 1856.

3. See letter 17.

4. Geneviève Halévy (1849–1926) married, first, Georges Bizet, then the lawyer Emile Straus. She was Proust's great friend and confidante.

5. M. and Mme Williams were having construction work done, and Proust obviously suffered from the noise.

6. The Count Robert de Montesquiou (1855–1921) was a man of letters and friend of Proust, a dandy and a model for the character of Baron de Charlus [in *In Search of Lost Time*].

7. He is thinking of Bagnoles-de-l'Orne, a spa town in Normandy, 'a home where you have memories of your family'. Proust also mentions the family home of Mme Williams in Le Vésinet.

8. *Portraits of Painters* was published in 1896 by Heugel and later included in *Pleasures and Days*, published by Calmann-Lévy on June 12, 1896.

9. From 1900 to 1912, Proust published numerous articles in *Le Figaro*, which makes the dating of this letter tricky. It could be either from 1909, after the publication of *Pastiches*, or from 1912 after that of excerpts from *Swann's Way*.

10. 'Prométhée triomphant' [Prometheus triumphant], an oratorio for solo voices and chorus set to a poem by Paul Reboux. Performed in concert on Friday, December 17, 1909, conducted by [Eberhard] Schwickerath. Reynaldo Hahn and a few French friends attended the concert and the banquet that followed it.

11. This occurred on September 30, 1914 (information kindly supplied by Mme Nathalie Mauriac-Dyer; M. Proust, *Correspondance*, vol. 13, p. 305). [To be mentioned in the army's *ordre du jour* signified that one was being honoured for one's courage or devotion to duty.]
[*Military service review board*: the meaning of Proust's own term is unclear. He speaks of a *conseil de contre-réforme*, which

did not exist as such. A *conseil de réforme*, however, was a body charged with examining soldiers who might be declared unfit to serve. Proust has added the word *contre* (against). He uses this same formulation in another letter, one written February 12, 1915, in which he says: 'My brother, since the first day, has been in great danger, but actually so far has escaped everything and is doing well. I have a *conseil de contre-réforme* to pass, but have not yet been summoned' (letter to Jean-Louis Vaudoyer, *Correspondance générale*, vol. 4, p. 67).]

12. Alfred Agostinelli died May 30, 1914.

13. John 3:8.

14. Joachim Joseph Charles Henri (1875–1918), third count of Clary, son of Napoleon II's aide-de-camp, a friend of Proust, Lucien Daudet, and Montesquiou, presumably an inspiration to Proust for the *japonisant* part of *In Search*, but also a model for Baron de Charlus going blind, in *Time Found Again*. Clary was the author of *L'île du soleil couchant* [The island of the setting sun], published by Arthème Fayard in 1912, a novel about Japan cited by Marcel Proust in one of his letters of November 1912.

[Since Joachim Clary is mentioned in no fewer than eight letters of the present volume, we may say a little more about him. The following description is taken from a memoir by his friend, the English composer and suffragist Ethel Smyth, in her *Impressions That Remained – Memoirs of Ethel Smyth*

(Knopf, 1919). She had first known Clary as one of the 'enfants de la maison' in the English residence of the Empress Eugénie, wife of Napoleon III:

> I had first known Clary as a clever, good-looking, active, rather spoilt youth; now, though still a young man, he was a cripple, scarcely able to move hand or foot, his limbs twisted and gnarled with arthritis, in constant pain day and night, and totally blind. Yet his originality, his culture, his unconquerable sense of humour and, above all, his superb courage, made our friendship one of the assets of my life.

Ethel Smyth remarks that Clary's death was 'wholly unexpected'. (At the time she describes seeing Clary, she would have been in her late fifties, Clary about 41. He was to die the following year.)]

15. The letter is torn in places, and passages are missing.

16. Doctor Léon Faisans (1851–1922), often mentioned in Proust's correspondence. He was a specialist in respiratory illnesses and a physician at the Hôpital Beaujon.

17. June and July 1914, pages 48 and 52 of *La Nouvelle Revue Française,* excerpted from *In the Shadow of Young Girls in Flower* and *The Guermantes Way I.*

18. The poet Maurice Rostand and the painter Jacques-Emile Blanche were close friends, as was Proust, of Lucien Daudet. Each of them devoted a laudatory article to *Swann's Way.*

19. 'The cruel fates.' A verse from Virgil's *Aeneid*, 6:882, addressed to Marcellus, nephew of Augustus. [It is perhaps a reference to the war.]

20. Proust was envisaging at this point a work in three volumes; the second was to have included the present *In the Shadow of Young Girls in Flower* and *The Guermantes Way*, in shorter versions. The Bibliothèque nationale de France holds the proofs of this volume printed by Grasset.

21. This important revelation was omitted from the final version of *In Search of Lost Time*.

22. Title of a book of poems by Anna, Countess de Noailles.

23. What is Proust referring to here? Is he alluding to the play by Maeterlinck, to a poem by Mallarmé, or to a poem by his neighbour herself?

24. Respectively, Agrippa d'Aubigné, *Les tragiques*, 4; Paul Verlaine, *Sagesse*; Gérard de Nerval, 'Artémis' and 'El Desdichado', *Les Chimères*.

25. The reference is to *Pelléas and Mélisande*, the lyric drama by Maurice Maeterlinck and Claude Debussy.

26. Perhaps an allusion to the train trip to Balbec described in *In the Shadow of Young Girls in Flower*, which appeared in *La Nouvelle Revue Française* in 1914 and in which the

narrator, borne away by the train, watches a young milkmaid recede into the distance.

27. Reynaldo Hahn was in the Argonne at Vauquois in April 1915. Bertrand de Fénelon (1878–1914) died December 17, 1914, at Mametz. [Since this fact was obscured by contradictory rumours until it was declared official in March of the following year, Proust did not fully accept it until then.]

28. Mme Williams's brother, Lieutenant Alphonse Emile Georges Marcel Pallu (1882–1915) of the Third Regiment of Dragoons, died for France (thus designated) as a result of an illness contracted in the field, February 13, 1915, at Nantes.

29. The dentist's office was on the third floor, above Proust's apartment. His private apartment was on the fourth (that is, on the third floor above the mezzanine).

30. He is referring to the military doctor (see letter 19).

31. According to the Baedeker of 1914, 'First-class hotel in the Champs-Elysées, 55 Avenue de l'Alma and 101 Avenue des Champs-Elysées.' The Avenue de l'Alma is now the Avenue George V.

32. The Countess Wladimir Rehbinder, née Jacqueline Contéré de Monbrison (1871–1925), wrote fashion articles. She was earlier divorced from Count Jacques de Pourtalès (1858–1919).

33. Madame de La Béraudière was the mistress of [Henri,] Count Greffulhe. Proust found her 'charming, in every respect, and with great vivacity and frankness of spirit' (*Correspondance*, vol. 14, p. 165, 1915). According to Céleste Albaret, Mme de La Béraudière 'was at the feet of M. Proust and didn't know what to do to make him interested' (Céleste Albaret, *Monsieur Proust*, p. 194).

34. Proust must finally have seen Clary again before October 15, 1915, according to his *Correspondance*.

35. Proust writes, in a letter of August 7, 1915: 'I cannot move these days, awaiting a visit from the Major of which I do not know the day or the hour.' The visit took place on August 8 or 9.

36. The reference is to pages on roses, written by Mme Williams (but which have not come down to us). See letter 14.

37. Mme Terre [Earth] was evidently the person in charge of the construction or renovation work that was making him suffer so (see letters 21 and 23). [Napoleon's mother was known as 'Madame Mère'.]

38. Verlaine's 'a shiver of water on moss' comes from 'Listen to the Very Gentle Song', 1881, the sixteenth poem of collection 1 of *Sagesse*: 'Listen to the very gentle song / That weeps only to please you, / It is discreet, it is light: / A shiver of water over moss!'

39. Jean de Reszke (1850–1925), opera singer (tenor), Polish by birth, as was his brother Édouard (bass).

40. See note 25. Pelléas says, at the end of act 2, scene 1, 'The truth, the truth.' [The Wolff Agency (misspelled by Proust) was a German press agency, one of the major news agencies of the 19th and early 20th centuries.]

41. Concerning Mme Terre, see also letters 20 and 23.

42. This is a pastiche of the sonnet that appeared in 1833 in the collection *Mes heures perdues* [My lost hours] by Félix Arvers.

43. According to his *Correspondance* (vol. 14), in mid-October 1915, Proust saw Clary again twice.

44. Hahn arrived from Vauquois on November 11 or 12, 1915. He made use of that leave to give the first performance of *Le ruban dénoué*. [In the original, for 'in disarray' Proust puns, using the expression *en 'bataille'* (literally 'in battle' – with quotes around 'battle') to signal the pun.]

45. Baudelaire, *The Flowers of Evil*, 42, line 6.

46. Reynaldo was a fervent admirer of Thérésa [Emma Valladon, 1837–1913], queen of the café-concert. She sang *La terre* [The earth] (L'Eldorado, 1888), poem and music both by Jules Jouy, arranged by Léopold Gandolff. The poem

begins: 'Our nurse and our mama— / She is the earth: / Her flower and grain sprouting / Under the earth.' Proust evokes this song to make fun of Mme Terre – see letters 20 and 21. (Information kindly supplied by Benoît Duteurtre.) Proust had heard this singer at the Théâtre du Châtelet in 1888, in *Cendrillon*.

47. This confirms that Proust consulted musical scores. *Les Béatitudes* is by César Franck.

48. Anatole France wrote the preface to Proust's *Pleasures and Days* (Calmann-Lévy, 1896).

49. Robert de Montesquiou's *Les offrandes blessées: Elégies guerrières* [Wounded offerings: War elegies] was published by E. Sansot in June 1915. Ida Rubinstein (1885–1960) was a celebrated Russian-born dancer and actress. This reading must have taken place on Wednesday, December 20, 1916, at the Théâtre Sarah Bernhardt. This letter can therefore be dated Tuesday the 19th.

50. Pierre Frondaie, novelist, playwright, and poet, used Anatole France's first novel, *The Crime of Sylvestre Bonnard*, as the basis for a four-act play which premiered at the Théâtre Antoine either December 2 or 20, 1916, according to different sources. [In his phrase 'the "acta Sanctorum" of the Learned Bollandistes', Proust is quoting from memory (with his own choices of capitalization) from France's novel: 'at the hour when the mice will dance by moonlight before the

Acta Sanctorum of the learned Bollandistes.' A Bollandiste was a member of a learned society founded by the Jesuit and hagiographer Jean Bolland. The *Acta Sanctorum* were the *Lives of the Saints*, of which Bolland was the first author and compiler.]

51. This play, adapted from Anatole France's novella *Crainquebille*, was first performed in 1903 starring Lucien Guitry at the Théâtre de la Renaissance in Paris. [*Crainquebille* is the story of a street peddler unjustly jailed and an orphan boy who befriends him on his release. It was also adapted for silent film by Jacques Feyder in 1921.]

52. A. Demar-Latour: *Ce qu'ils ont détruit: La cathédrale de Reims bombardée et incendiée en septembre 1914* [What they destroyed: The cathedral of Reims bombed and burned in September 1914], Paris, Éditions practiques et documentaires ([1915?], 64 pp.). [It is possible, though not certain, that this is the book Mme Williams lent to Proust. As for the year of its appearance, the book itself contains no publication date, and sources, such as library catalogues, variously give 1914 and 1915.]

53. In *The Crime of Sylvestre Bonnard*, the princess (not countess) Trépof presents Sylvestre Bonnard with the manuscript of *The Golden Legend*, which he has been coveting, secreted within a hollowed-out log. Proust cites the same passage in a letter of May 1913 to Mme Schéikevitch (*Correspondance*, vol. 12, p. 173).

54. The compatriot is perhaps Walter Berry, President of the Franco-American Chamber of Commerce and a friend of Proust.

55. The source of the phrase is in fact the 11th-century monk Raoul Glaber.

56. [Because Proust refers to the death of Clary's mother, which occurred March 11, 1917, and because Clary himself, who died May 8, 1918, is evidently still alive, this letter must have been written sometime between those two dates. Proust had been out of touch with Blanche, whom he mentions here, before April 10, 1918. He is presumably back in touch with him if he contemplated sending him the carnations. A possible date for this letter, therefore, would be sometime in the month extending from mid-April to mid-May.]

Index

WORKS AND CHARACTERS OF PROUST

WORKS AND CHARACTERS OF PROUST